Rookie Read-About® **Science**

It's a Good Thing There Are
Bees

by Lisa M. Herrington

Content Consultant
Elizabeth Case DeSantis, M.A. Elementary Education
Julia A. Stark Elementary School, Stamford, Connecticut

Reading Consultant
Jeanne Clidas, Ph.D.
Reading Specialist

Children's Press®
An Imprint of Scholastic Inc.
New York Toronto London Auckland Sydney
Mexico City New Delhi Hong Kong
Danbury, Connecticut

Library of Congress Cataloging-in-Publication Data
Herrington, Lisa M., author.
It's a good thing there are bees/by Lisa M. Herrington.
      pages cm. — (Rookie read-about science)
Summary: "Introduces the reader to bees and explains the roles they play in the
environment."— Provided by publisher.
Audience: Ages 3-6.
ISBN 978-0-531-22359-8 (library binding: alk. paper) — ISBN 978-0-531-22831-9 (pbk.: alk. paper)
   1. Bees—Juvenile literature. 2. Honeybee—Juvenile literature. I. Title. II. Title: It is a
good thing there are bees. III. Series: Rookie read-about science.

   SF523.5.H47 2015
   595.79'9—dc23   2014014962

Produced by Spooky Cheetah Press
Design by Keith Plechaty

© 2015 by Scholastic Inc.

Printed in China 62

SCHOLASTIC, CHILDREN'S PRESS, ROOKIE READ-ABOUT®, and associated logos
are trademarks and/or registered trademarks of Scholastic Inc.

1 2 3 4 5 6 7 8 9 10 R 24 23 22 21 20 19 18 17 16 15

Photographs © 2015: Photos ©: Dreamstime: 27 bottom (Alexandru Razvan
Cofaru), 27 top right (Gianluigi Becciu), 7, 31 center bottom (Jan Richter), 15 (Milada
Kozlovska); Getty Images/Florin Tirlea: 20; iStockphoto/mirecca: 4; Minden Pictures/
Dietmar Nill: 28 top; Science Source/Scott Camazine: 23; Shutterstock, Inc.:
3 top left (Dani Vincek), 29 (Darios), 27 top left (Dionisvera), cover (Kitsadakron_
Photography), 30 bottom, 31 center top (Nikola Spasenoski), 16 (Ti Santi), 3 top right
(Tischenko Irina), 3 bottom (Tsekhmister); Superstock, Inc.: 8, 31 bottom (Gerard Lacz
Images), 12 (Heidi & Hans-Jurgen Koch), 19, 31 top (LOOK-foto), 28 bottom (Minden
Pictures), 24 (NHPA); Thinkstock: 11 (George Doyle), 30 top left (HappyToBeHomeless),
30 top right (PapaBear), 28 center (SweetCrisis).

Table of Contents

4

It's a Good Thing...

A bee makes a buzzing sound as its wings beat quickly. The bee's buzz scares a lot of people. They are afraid of getting stung. But it is a good thing there are bees!

A bee can flap its wings more than 11,000 times a minute.

Bees are nature's busy helpers. They sip a sweet juice called **nectar** from flowers. They use nectar to make honey.

FUN FACT!

Honeybees have to visit about two million flowers to make just 1 pound (0.5 kilogram) of honey!

Some bees carry pollen in special spots on their back legs.

Bees collect **pollen** from flowers for food. They spread pollen to other flowers. This helps flowers make seeds. New plants grow. Many of the fruits, vegetables, and nuts we eat come from those plants.

FUN FACT!

A bee's body is covered in tiny hairs. Pollen sticks to the hairs.

Bees also make wax. Many things that we use every day are made with beeswax. They include candles, crayons, and even makeup.

FUN FACT!

Bees sting to defend themselves. Wasps, skunks, and bears are some of their enemies. Not all bees die after they sting, but a honeybee does.

wings

head

antennas

thorax

abdomen

leg

What Are Bees?

Bees are **insects**. They have three body parts: head, thorax, and abdomen. They also have six legs and four wings. They use their two antennas to smell.

Bees have two big eyes and three small eyes. They see more colors than people can see. This lets them find nectar in flowers.

More than 20,000 kinds of bees buzz around our planet. They live everywhere except for the coldest places.

Most bees are yellow with black or brown stripes. They can even be blue or green.

A blue carpenter bee feeds on a flower.

Life in the Hive

Some bees live alone. Others live in a large group called a **colony**. A colony of honeybees builds homes called hives. A hive can hold thousands of bees.

Bees often build their hives in old trees.

There are three kinds of honeybees. One queen bee rules the hive. She is the biggest bee of all. The queen's job is to lay eggs that will become new bees.

The male bees are called drones. The females are worker bees. The hive is made up mostly of worker bees.

FUN FACT!

At the hive, a bee does a special dance to tell others where to find flowers.

queen

cell

The hive is a busy place. Inside, worker bees use wax from their bodies to make tiny holes. They are called honeycomb cells. Honey and eggs are stored in the cells.

Worker bees bring nectar and pollen back to the hive. They make honey and raise the young. They also clean and guard the hive.

FUN FACT!

In one day, a worker bee can visit about 1,000 flowers!

How Bees Grow

Bees begin life as eggs. The queen bee lays an egg in a cell in the hive. After a few days, the egg hatches. It is now a larva. Worker bees feed the larva honey and pollen. The larva grows.

FUN FACT!

Queen bees can live about five years, but most bees die after a few weeks.

larva

Then the bees seal the cell with wax. Inside, the larva changes shape. Soon it becomes a grown bee. The bee chews through the wax. It is now ready to become a busy member of the hive.

FUN FACT!

During winter, bees eat their stored honey. They huddle together to stay warm.

From pollinating flowers to making honey, bees can help us in many ways. It's a good thing there are bees!

One out of every three bites of food we eat is grown with help from honeybees.

Bees Are Good For...

...making honey.

...making beeswax.

...spreading pollen to flowers.

Bumblebees build their nests in groups underground.

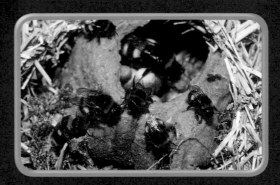

Carpenter bees live alone. They get their name because they can chew through wood to build their nests.

Leafcutter bees snip through leaves on plants. They use the pieces to build their nests.

Feature Fun

Beekeepers build hives in wooden boxes. They raise bees for their honey and wax. Some also raise bees to help farmers grow their crops. Special clothes protect beekeepers from stings.

RIDDLES

Q. Why did the bee get a trophy?

A. *Because it won the spelling bee!*

Q. What did the bee say after returning to the hive?

A. *Honey, I'm home!*

Creature Feature Fun

Which habitat is right for bees?

A

B

Answer: B. Bees need to live where there are plants and flowers.

Plant Bee-Friendly Flowers!

Honeybees have been dying off. If bees are in trouble, then our crops can suffer, too. Scientists think a virus may be one of the reasons bees are getting sick. They are working to help them. Kids can help, too. You can plant gardens with bee-friendly flowers, such as daisies, poppies, sunflowers, and asters.

Glossary

colony (KOL-uh-nee): large group of insects that live together

insects (IN-sects): animals with three main body parts and six legs

nectar (NEK-tur): sweet liquid that bees collect from flowers and turn into honey

pollen (POL-uhn): tiny yellow grains that help flowers make new seeds

Index

Facts for Now

Visit this Scholastic Web site for more information on bees:
www.factsfornow.scholastic.com
Enter the keyword **Bees**

About the Author

Lisa M. Herrington writes many books and articles for kids. She is thankful to bees for the honey she loves to put in her tea! Lisa lives in Trumbull, Connecticut, with her husband, Ryan, and daughter, Caroline.